A Listless Daughter

Jalisha Gilliam

VMH Vikki M. Hankins™ Publishing
www.vmhpublishing.com

Copyright © 2018 by Jalisha Gilliam

Without limiting the rights under copyright reserved above, no part of this publication may be reproduced, stored in or introduced into a retrieval system, or transmitted, in any form or by any means.

Book Cover Design: Vikki Jones
Book Cover Image: Shutterstock
Interior Design: VMH Publishing

VMH Vikki M. Hankins™ Publishing is a registered trademark, and the publisher of this work. For information about the company or for bulk purchases, please contact VMH Publishing at info@vmhpublishing.com.

Publisher's Note:

The publisher is not responsible for the content of this book nor websites, or social media pages (or their content) that are not owned by the publisher.

Manufactured in the United States of America

10 9 8 7 6 5 4 3 2 1

Hardback ISBN: 978-1-947928-52-7
Paperback ISBN: 978-1-947928-50-3

This book is a dedication to my father,
Mr. Jerry Terrell.
For being the kind of dad that every girl should have.

P.S.,
To You, My Big Daddy For Being My First love!

Contents

Chapter 1
Reminiscent of Daddy 11

Chapter 2
My First Heartbreak 23

Chapter 3
Pointless Opinions 35

Chapter 4
Our Daddy 47

Chapter 5
Growing Pains 53

Chapter 6
A Daughter's Desolation 69

Chapter 7
A Daughter's Deplore 71

Chapter 8
Gone Too Soon 81

Chapter 9
Gone Unapologetic 97

Chapter 10
When the Heart Heals 103

Introduction

I bet there is not one woman who can tell me they did not think their dad was the shit growing up. However, this is only accurate if he was active in their life, because if not, then to hell with him. My father was the first man that meant the world to me. When I looked at him, all I could do was smile, because his love was like no other love on this earth! So, yes, as a young girl growing up, I thought "father" was the definition of love. Hell! I went through a phase of not wanting a boyfriend, because in my eyes, another man could never amount to his standards. Everything I could ever want was already given to me, so the "boyfriend" thing was pointless.

The bond my father and I shared was so unique, and I knew it could never be replaced. My dad was the true definition of a positive dad.

Chapter 1

Reminiscent of Daddy

Yes, I feel like a special daughter who had the experience of a lifetime to have had a father as genuine as I did. Most young girls do not have that positive male role model in their lives teaching them how to cope with situations that may come their way. My father may not be here physically anymore, but he sure as hell would be smiling that crooked smile if he could see how well all those loquacious conversations really paid off. Yep, Daddy, I listened. I remember all the silly quotes that you spoke.

My dad was Mr. Man of the Hour, too sweet to be sour, kill a rock and put a brick in the hospital, fine as wine, and smooth as frog hair! Can you say hilarious! Jerry David Terrell was the man, honey. Anyone who knew him was aware that he was going to have you cracking up something serious. The jokester of all times, baby, his cool self. Not only was he funny, but he was giving as well. If you asked for anything, he would reply, "Shit, I was going to ask you the same thing." A mess I tell you!

He was well known in the Sylvan Road Community, and when I say known, I really mean that literally. Older folks, especially women, loved him. He repeated his same old line, "Don't nothing get old but clothes and money, honey." The people who ran the five stores in the community also loved him, because he played the Georgia Lottery consistently. He also bought his Cherry Skoal and shopped at the stores all the time. The list really can go on and on. My dad was the best!

All my young life, I enjoyed the love and time spent with my father, because daddy's little girl was the most special gift God could give to him. It was so hard for him to tell his baby girl no.

Men pride their daughters in every way possible, and instill in their brains that they should think of themselves as being the brightest apples at the top of the tree. If a man wants me, then he is going to do whatever it takes to get me. Only the scared boys who lack confidence will be too timid to climb high up, because they doubt their ability to man up for my challenges. Everyone knows boys are scared of getting hurt, so they choose the rotten apples from the bottom, because they are much easier to manipulate. But, not to worry, all the beautiful apples at the top continue to wait patiently for the night man to climb his brave behind to the top of that tree and get them (ahem, Pete Wentz).

Every man wants their daughter to have that kind of knowledge stored in their minds. Settling for a *man* is the goal, not the ones who still have a *boy* mentality.

My father and I always played around, and eventually, the subject of boys came up. Right then and there our conversations would begin.

Thinking back on everything my dad told me as a kid cracks the grown woman in me up! My entire life, all he wanted was for me to know my worth, and be able to love myself regardless of any flaw I may have had. He didn't want me to get all excited when a guy told me

I'm beautiful. That was something I would already know from the start.

Most men could never be able to work up the nerves to have a conversation about sex to their daughters. They are too busy trying to make sure they don't engage in it all. What's the point of trying to shelter it away from her, when in reality, she's going to adventure it for herself one day. So, he decided to fill me in. In the beginning, I didn't quite comprehend what he was implying, but now it's hilarious to me. I mean, really, Dad, you compared sex to food. What a way to put it down to me! He was so unique about everything.

These are the revised diary entries I wrote about coming up as a young girl on time spent with my Big Daddy. Let the reminiscing begin...

September 3, 2001

Today is my birthday, so Uncle Walt is taking me to Dad's so I can give him our new address. Dad gives his baby all the presents she wants, duh.

December 15, 2001

Today I am going over to Dad's house. He is taking me shopping and getting me whatever I want, we will have so much fun!

My mistake, it seems as if Daddy has lost the little brains God gave him, because he didn't freaking come! Well, so what, I might be exaggerating, or whatever, so what. He is totally tripping and slipping. What he needs to do is get his mind right. I'm so angry right now. Daddy used to always talk 'bout how dogs get mad, and humans get angry. Well, I'm mad, Daddy. Guess I'm a dog, huh? Seriously, though, hurry and come get me so we can spend time 2gether!

May 28, 2002

Today I am so excited, because my favorite man is coming to pick me up. We are celebrating me graduating from the fifth grade at Mary McLeod Bethune Elementary School. I told him, "Even though I'm getting older and I'm gonna start dating boys soon, I will always be your baby girl."

He looked at me, smiled, and said, "Hotta Motty, and you better know it, girl." Daddy means so much to me, I am so lucky to be his one and only daughter.

October 2, 2002

On this day, I wrote, "My dad is pitiful," very big on four sheets of my diary paper. Wondering what he done? Probably didn't give me what I wanted when I asked for it. I was such a spoiled little brat. So what!

January 1, 2005

I spent New Year's with Dad, and it was wonderful! We counted the peach drop, and when we got to one, I took his favorite wine, Verdi Green Apple, and drank it. We hugged and told one another, "Happy New Year's!" I was happy to spend it with him. When I grow up, he's gonna be mad I won't be his baby girl anymore. My future husband is gonna be mad, too, because my dad and I are gonna talk shit to his ass!

We stayed up until 3 a.m. talking about who I was going to be, and how I better not let a man run over me, same old, same old. Daddy's I tell ya. Daddy better know I will be a man's queen one day, geesh!

April 8, 2005

Dad is coming to get me!

My cousins and I went to the movies to see *Beauty Shop*. It was off the chain. I hope to get my own salon like Queen Latifah.

We all went back to my Dad's mother-in-law's house, but when we got there, she was angry for no reason. I called Dad so we could dip. Henrietta, my dad's wife, was mad, but me and Dad continued to have a good rest of the night. (Oh, and yes, I will have my own salon one day, watch it, baby).

April 9, 2005

Dad and I are just chilling. We trippin' off these two ugly people walking by, and all that funny junk. I enjoy every moment we have together, because when he is gone, which will be a long time from now, I will have amazing memories. Dad is, like, literally the coolest dad ever, not saying it because he's my dad, but because he is.

April 10, 2005

    Today I have to leave Dad's house, our Spring Break is over, so we have to return to school. Every single time I am with Dad we have the best time ever. Maybe because he agrees to everything I say. He says, "When you get a man, make sure he do the same thing I do now." He crazy as hell, but in a good way. I love him to pieces.

    I hope I marry a rich man, ayyye! He'll take care of me and Daddy. Hotta motty!

May 6, 2005

    Today Daddy called me and told me to come get some money for my 8th grade prom, and for sure, I said, "Ok!" He gave me $150, even though I thought he said $160, it was cool, though. I gave him a hug, and as I was leaving, Henrietta called me to the back room and gave me $60 more, and told me to enjoy myself. She is so good to me; our relationship is great. I love her, she is a great stepmom.

I'll be cute tomorrow ayyeee!

May 20, 2005

Today is Dad's 53rd birthday, and also the day I graduate from 8th grade at John F. Kennedy Middle School. I'm ready to start Benjamin K. Mays High School and join their cheerleading team. Dad was so happy to share his day with me. Dad and I will turn up after I'm done getting my party on with my friends. Watch out, high school, here I come!

June 3, 2005

I called Dad and he is coming to pick me up. We are going to have fun as usual. I'm Daddy's little princess.

June 5, 2005

Today I came back from Dad's house, and I am shocked to see he only gave me $80. That's nothing compared to what he normally gives me, but hey, at least I still got cash, no biggie. Next time I will count it out right then and there. I mean, I am his baby girl, and my items are more expensive now.

June 13, 2005

I went to Dad's house to take a nap. When I woke up, Hennetta and I walked to the store, and we saw Dad walking up. He went on in the house, he didn't look well. Hennetta and I walked on, and when we returned, he told me to go on home because he wasn't feeling too well. He gave me, like, $260, and I didn't even really want it, because I was worried about him. Seeing Dad down was scary to me. I hope he gets better soon.

September 3, 2005

Today is my 15th birthday. I had on this Ecko Red skirt outfit, it was red, black, white, and blue. Dad came to pick me up so he could show his beautiful princess off. We all went over to Hennetta's son, Charles, house for a barbeque (for some odd reason I don't think he cares for me, but anyway). Everyone sang "Happy Birthday" to me and gave me cards and cash. I really enjoyed myself this birthday. We returned back home and Hennetta got tired and went to sleep. Dad and I stayed up. He pulled out a card and it had $200 in it. He kissed my cheeks and gave me the biggest hug.

Of course, we had the talk about boys, and how at this age they try to manipulate pretty young ladies like myself to have sex with them. That's just Daddy being a daddy again. He said, "Trust me, no nappy headed little boys will get you, Princess." Him and his quotes, man, geesh, it's my birthday.

"I'll be careful, Daddy." That's my daddy, man! Night, night, my diary, talk to you whenever.

Chapter 2

My First Heartbreak

All these diary entries really have taken my mind back down memory lane. They have me smiling from ear to ear.

My father tried to fit a sex conversation into every sentence him and I would have at times. Even when I didn't understand what he was trying to imply. As adolescents, our mothers and fathers tell us stories about the birds and the bees, but my story was a little on the sharing side. He explained to me that I should never let a nappy headed boy have sex with me, because then he would think that he has some sort of authority over me. Especially never let him put his bare mouth on anything I am drinking, because he may be going around putting his bare mouth on other little girls, and that could cause me to have a nasty disease. So, of course, I was always remained attentive to those conversations and lived up to those rules, because my daddy told me that.

As time went by, middle school was in full effect. The sex education class I was enrolled in sounded familiar to me.

Oh goodness! I remember this like yesterday. The boys would call me names like stingy, stuck-up, mean girl, fake teacher, fake police, control girl, and anything else in the same category as not sharing and being in charge. Even the teachers would laugh, because they knew I was not giving anyone anything, unless I could be in charge of it. I often treated some of the girls the same way, too, if I did not care for them much.

I could not wait to get to my daddy, because he had some explaining to do! I told him, "I was called 'stingy, mean, stuck-up, and tight,' and you were really talking about sex the entire time!" My dad did not know how much I defended myself to those boys, like I was some kind of bad person.

He said, "You right. I sure was!"

"I did not share with boys because I thought they would give me a disease and all that mess."

He said, "Girl, you growing up now, these boys will try to have sex with you and another girl at the same time, not caring who else she may be sleeping with. Always use protection whenever you decide, but hopefully that is a long time from now. But, seriously, you can catch a disease that you will never get rid of. Boys lie all the time, trust me, I know. Hell, I was a boy once before in my life, even when I was supposed to be a man. That is another story, though, we talking about you as of now."

At that very moment, I realized it was ok. My dad really did not lie to me, he was protecting me. Standing up for myself was never a problem. My dad made sure his baby girl was strong, not weak-minded and gullible. Being a girl in the world made me no less than a man, I am and will always be in control of anything that may come my way.

I made it clear that his princess was up on all the games guys talk. My dad and I literally talked about anything, and he understood where I was coming from, then we would move past it. Except this one devastating memory.

Since we're going down memory lane, oh my goodness!

The time had come for me to tell him all those sex education conversations we had repeatedly had finally become reality! Not only was he two years late, since I had lost my virginity at the age of 15, but now I was only 17, in the 12th grade, and about to have a child. That was the most heartbreaking thing I could have ever let come out of my mouth, especially since we talked about everything all the time. For me to break this secret was the worst.

I sat him down on the couch and said, "Daddy, I love you."

He replied, "I just gave you some money, plus you know you want to run for Miss 12th Grade, so no, I will only give you $100 or less."

I started laughing and said, "No, silly, you're about to be a grandfather!"

He looked at me directly in my eyes and responded, "How is that possible when you have to have sex to have a baby? Plus, you have not brought no so called 'boyfriend' to meet up with

Big Daddy, girl, and I damn sure don't recall him asking me to ask for your hand in marriage. Until that happens, that is when you can come to me and tell me I have a got damn grandbaby on the way, sista girl!" He got up, walked in his room, came back out, paused, opened the door again, and slammed it so hard the floor shook!

My face was full of tears. I was completely in awe! Not once did he glimpse or glance at me on his way out the door. Only thing I heard was him cursing every other word. "What the fuck? This shit got to be a damn joke! Oh, hell to the fucking no!"

I watched my father walk away from me for the very first time in my life. He had never done such a thing! Never in my life of 17 years of living have I ever endured so much hurt on this earth! Definitely not by the man to whom I love so very much. This was very disappointing to me, because I felt that the man I always depended on had turned his back against me over one fault.

All I could do was run to the bathroom and cry.

Henrietta treated me as if I was her own ever since I can remember. She was banging on the door trying to get in. I was so hurt, and I just sat there. I could not bare to open the door at that moment. Minutes later, I walked into the living room, where she was rolling up her hair as usual. There, she explained that my father was upset and hurt all in one. "His baby girl is not as innocent as he thought she was, so hang in there, he will come around." Her and I talked some more before I went home.

I would not speak to my father for months to come.

Two months passed, and my father and I still had not spoken to one another. I had an attitude as if I didn't care, but I knew deep inside it was eating me alive. How could the man I love turn his back on me? But, it's life, so if he don't talk, I won't say a word.

On one particular day, I spoke to my Aunt Tudy. She came over to chit chat, but I was not feeling so good. She asked if I had spoken to my father, and I told her I hadn't.

She said, "Girl, you know you got your stubbornness from your dad. Get on in the car and let's go for a ride."

I was down for it. So, as we were driving, the scenery became familiar and I yelled out, "Oh no, you not taking me over to his house, Tudy."

She started laughing and replied, "Girl, you can't get out, so hey." I was so mad, but then again, I had this excitement in my stomach as well, because I knew my dad would be happy to see me. Things would get back to normal.

Once we pulled into the apartment complex, my dad and his friends were sitting outside listening to Tupac. His music was blasting! My dad would always have the song "California Love" on repeat until someone demanded him to change it. I walked over and sat on his lap, and took his hat off his head, then spoke to everyone under the tree. Of course, they all started talking at one time, because they had not seen me since I became pregnant. Mr. Floyd made a comment saying, "If it's a boy, he is going to be with me and your pops, we were cracking up about it. Or, if it's a girl, we gon' help her with cheerleading practice like we did with you." That just made me smile, because obviously he had been thinking about me. We just laughed! Everyone was talking and talking, and I had yet to hear one word from my dad's mouth. I got up and went into the house so I could speak to Henrietta, and she already had a plate of food ready for me.

She asked me, "Has your father acknowledged you any?"

I replied, "No. He's being as stubborn as ever."

She started yelling at my dad, and he said, "She didn't speak to Big Daddy, so, hey, you know it's cool with me, I won't lose no sleep." That shit made me so freaking angry, so we left.

Tudy said, "You and him are both alike, so you might as well let it go." I didn't want to hear that, I was just ready to go, so we did.

Finally, I returned back to my house, all alone. I was sad and emotional. I thought my dad really didn't love his baby girl anymore. I cried myself to sleep, and when I woke up, I called my child's father over so he could come pick me up. We relaxed so my mind could be clear.

Months passed on, and it was the day of my baby shower. It was January of 2009. I received a call from my father. At first, I was hesitant, because we had not spoken to each other since the summer of 2008 when I left his house. So, I answered, and he said, "Hey, enjoy your day."

I replied, "Ok, thank you. I sure will!" I then hung up the phone. I just laughed and was like, whatever.

The time had finally come. My son was born on February 12, 2009, in the morning. My father walked into the room, and my face lit up like a candle. My heart was racing 80 miles per hour (seemingly), and all I wanted to do was squeeze my father's neck. Despite us being all angry at one another, that did not matter to me at that moment. The pain I had recently endured while giving birth to my son hours earlier was nothing like the pain I felt in my heart while my father and I had not spoken.

My mom, Lesia, and sister, Nikkeenna, stepped out of the room, and as soon as they did, my father stood up over me and stated, "Even with us not talking, that was a lesson for you, baby girl. True enough, I was angry at the fact my princess was going to be a teen mom, but at the same time, I wanted to turn that into a lesson on your behalf. Any time a man gets angry at you for something you have done, sit back and evaluate his actions. He will either act out and blame you for his doings, or sit you down and confront you like a man should. You are to never go running, begging, or trying to plead your case. Let him keep his distance, and then he will realize, no matter what the issue may have been, you can work it out. He will notice that you're strong and can stand on your own, with or without him. That will make him love you even more."

I just said, "Ok, Daddy."

The nurse came into the room to check on me, and let me know my baby would return in 5 to 6 more minutes. He was taken away moments before my dad arrived. Shortly after, the nurse walked in the room with my son, Jamarcus, and my father's eyes were as bright as the sun. He was nervous to hold him, so Nikkeenna just placed him in his arms. Not even a minute later, my father bucked his eyes wide yelling, "Get him, he is pulling away!" We all began to laugh.

All that time had passed, and I sat back and realized how silly it was to not talk to my father, just because he was not talking to me. I had to step up and be the bigger person, because when it was all said and done, I could never get back the time I lost.

Chapter 3

Pointless Opinions

I remember how my father would always tell me not to judge my friends or associates, because I could never know what they were going through. However, I would shrug off his comments, because growing up, I thought what I thought, and that was that!

I constantly think about how I interpret situations as an adult, and how others should interpret them as well.

How in the world could a "man" have the audacity to falsely claim an unborn child, by the same chick he had unprotected sex with? At least say it's a possibility, even if you're sure she let someone else shoot her plug up. Man up, do not miss precious moments. Let me break it down into terminology everyone can relate to. Check me out!

If a man does not feel the need to actually raise a child a woman created, then he should not go sticking his gun in random bodies.

It doesn't matter if she is enjoying his gun along with him, there are consequences. The bullet he releases into her has found its other piece of the missing puzzle. What the bullet and puzzle piece are going to do is combine into one and become an embryo, then a fetus, and then finally a baby. Babies do not have the intelligence to think of consequences, but the parents do, and this is the price they pay for caressing the trigger hand. Now it has fired off, but he claims he's not the daddy, though?

Going back to the excitement she was feeling when everything was good, not only did they make each other climax at the same time, but they were so caught up in the moment that the two climaxers joined as one to create life. How great is that!

Which category would they want their baby girl to fall under: the girl whose father was in her life, or the girl who had no father in her life? The decision was totally up to them.

When a father is not present in a young ladies' life, she will feel either two emotions: she will lust after love, or she will think men will never amount to much. Then, she will get tough, and conclude to not let men in her life at all.

Her father was out of the picture, so she latched onto the first man that came her way. A man has never shown her love, so she is soaking up every ounce of attention she can. Any little thing that he does is perfect, because to her, he can do no wrong. However, she will be totally blindsided whenever he truly wrongs her. And he won't be blindsided at all when she finally breaks but remains by his side, because he knows her background, and knows how important it is for her to have his love. Playing on her intelligence is all fun and games to him. Eventually, she will figure it out, but when she does, she will discard it, because she is just hoping he will get it together. There will come a point when exhaustion consumes her, so, out the door she'll go. He'll play his mind games, though, and that will lead her right back into his arms. He manipulates the fact that he's nothing like her father, because he will stay, and he will always do good by her. It lures her in again, because he knows how weak she is for him, and he knows she will soak up his bullshit like a sponge. She is left numb to the real love she is missing from her father, that could never be replaced. She settles and deals with it, as long as he apologizes, he will always have her by his side, even through the worst times.

Which is the complete opposite from the woman who does not care if she has a man, period. Her father was not present, but she saw her mom work hard and struggle to give her the things she needed. Even if she gives a man a try, the first wrong thing he does to her, she will drop him like a bad habit! Her pride is all she has and she refuses to struggle through life as she saw her mom struggle, with a lazy guy by her side. Her mom was the one working, cleaning, buying, asking, and providing, while that poor excuse of a boyfriend watched her and didn't do one thing. Independence is looking very good to this woman.

She constantly thought of her father not coming around and the other man her mom was with was just as worthless as her father was. To hell with men! Even if they got a shot at a relationship with her, it would not last, because men are all the same to her. Blocking out love is a natural relaxation she has found within herself. Her only focus is success, because there is nothing a man can do for her that she cannot do for herself. Her self-worth is way up, so if any man wants her, they better lift her up. Her goals are set and in full effect, baby.

Differentiating from the girl who did not have her father in her life, but was lucky enough to still have that positive male role model (brother, uncle, cousin, step dad, granddad, relative's significant other, etc.), her biological father was out of the picture, but she sure as hell did not miss out on the love and wise words from a man.

Unlike the young girl who has a dad present, but only showers her with material things. He does not have time to play around and bond with her, all he has to do is kiss her on the forehead, or cheek, and tell her to "Get whatever she wants." Like that will prevent her from doing things with guys to get her all the items Daddy's already giving her. Wrong! Later in life, it will only have her taking on the male role. Showering her boyfriend or husband with gifts, because she does not have time either. However, she knows he will keep loving her. Why? All thanks to Daddy, all he did was say he loved her, worked, and gave, gave, gave. Even when he could not make it to a sporting event or recital, or just hurt her, he gave her material things. And now she does the same.

Maybe she'll go another route and bring home a big-time drug dealer to meet Daddy. All Dad did was give her gifts she wanted, so of course she is attracted to guys with the fast money. She had everything growing up with Daddy in her life, but the most important thing he could not buy her was the bond between a daddy and daughter.

A bond money could never buy.

A young lady may have a father who was not present, but chose to not let that dictate how she became. She knows her heart is set on a family, so going on about life the correct way and letting love find her is easy.

That is why these women made the choices they made when it came to men. It is not because of what they were brought up by. As a grown person, you are entitled to your own actions and held accountable for anything and everything you do. You know wrong from right, how to stand, and how to act in situations that you know aren't right. It is up to you to deal, or delete.

So, in actuality, there is no certain way a woman turns out if her father is present in her life or not. She is a woman who feels as if she has nothing, but still has the ability to build herself up, and the strength to hold her head high, knowing she is a strong woman! Just like the girl who has it all can learn to become independent, and does not need handouts from anyone. Things we go through are up to us. We are human and can grasp to other's strong points. Making one's insecurities disappear is a deed we should all hop on board with.

Summing it up to the girl who had it all. A father and brother giving her all the things she could want, and all the long talks about the curious little boys. This girl is very relatable to me. Why? Because this young lady is me.

Am I still dealing with the cons that come along with being Daddy's little princess? No! I am not saying it is his fault, but the actions I made were because being an adult was all new to me. Let's be honest for a second. Being your dad's only child, and your mom's last baby, the word responsibility is nowhere in sight. Anytime I needed anything, all I had to do was go to them. They would not let me go anywhere without getting my hair done, my nails done, giving me extra money in my pockets, and anything of that sort. So, paying bills, such as: rent, mortgage, life insurance, water, lights, gas, phone, health insurance, etc., was unfamiliar to me. I did not have to pay them.

I realized it was not cute to be fully grown still saying comments like, "I don't know how to cook. I don't do this, or that." Even when it comes down to the boyfriend and Daddy conversation. All my life, my dad told me a man should do this and that.

My Confessions

Many young girls don't get the chance to be spoiled by everyone, but I had it good on both ends. My stepsister may not have the same mother, but she is my sister forever. Taprine was just excited to have a baby sister finally, because her mom had two boys. Her father was deceased at birth, so my dad was the only father she ever knew. She was Dad's first princess, way before I was ever thought about. So, when I came around, she was ready to dress me up and flaunt me around in the jaunty clothes she got for me. The love she had for my father was unbreakable, no one could ever tell her he was her stepdad. That was her daddy way before he was mine, in her voice (laughs aloud). Oh, how we laughed.

Sir was the best stepbrother a girl could have! Sir and I had a beautiful relationship being. He told me how my father loved him and taught him to love all kids, people, and music. My dad always bragged on how smart he was, and hoped I accomplished life's great journeys, as he did. Sad to say how he was the one helping me and gave me pointers on how to just write from the heart. Now he has gone on to heaven (rest in peace, brother).

With Henrietta's last son, him and I never got the chance to build a relationship. That's life, and nothing is as perfect as it seems. My father and him were distant, but the love my dad had for him was real.

One conversation with my father stuck with me, and opened my mind to life situations I never thought of. Women are categorized in all aspects of a man's way of thinking. They will only do what you allow and tolerate. This guy I was dating had my dad's eyes wide open.

He had more qualities about himself that were far more relevant than material items could ever buy. My father loved that I had a man taking actions. Only a real man shows his skills off while out in public. A man is king of his castle, meaning he is already trained properly, making him fully groomed and ready to go.

When you walk, his position is to be on the outside of you, so no one tries to grab you. Or, just to be there to grab you if you slip off the sidewalk. He is opening up doors, walking in first to make sure you're safe. Right behind you while you're walking up the stairs, in case you lose your balance. Even in front of you as you're walking down so you will not fall forward, and be able to make it to the last step safely, without falling on your beautiful face, which he adores so. He will make sure you are walking right by his side, because you are his equal. No need to walk in front of him, even though he will love what he is seeing, because he is no better than you.

The both of you walking side-by-side is what a man wants. He's totally in love with the sight his peripheral is giving him, he could not have made a better decision on this one.

You are simply his trophy, the queen he has chosen to sit next to him. He put his prince mentalities away. It is you he sees complimenting him in ways he could never have imagined. After Daddy said that, it made sense. As long as he is treating me as a queen that's all that matters. Silver and gold have nothing on love and chivalry. The hell with the diamonds and bags, I will take the chivalry and love for $1,000, please, checkmate!

Chapter 4

Our Daddy

How in the hell could I have been so mean and bratty to a father with a heart of gold? I was so judgmental, and, like, as if, but my father taught me how to love the right way. To not like someone is not to not love them. We talk smack, but at the end of the day, the love is there.

Not only was my father's love unconditional, but it was just like that genuinely. An all-around stand-up guy in my eyes. I would always wonder why he told people he had all the kids, but they only saw him with me. On down the road, I discovered the love he shared with my siblings, even though they were not his biologically. My mom had 4 kids, and each of them appreciated his presence he graced them with.

My sister always supported me no matter what the case was. Mary was the baby of them all, so when my mom would leave for work, her and my father would watch ThunderCats. Entertaining her made her feel loved and special. Time spent with my dad was precious, and she valued that as she became an adult. She always told me, "He was my daddy before he was yours." We laughed about it.

Anytime you run into a hard situation, debt, or anything, she will be right by your side to love you with open arms. Be ready to get told a lesson, though. Jermen was the middle child, it took her a minute to warm up to my daddy, because her dad was active in her life. Mary and her shared the same father, but Mary did not mind at all, being that she was too young to understand another man being around. She felt as if he showed favoritism in them. In her mind, she thought he gave the oldest more. Not until she got older, she came to the realization that he truly did love them all. Nikkeena's father was not in her life, plus she was older, her belongings were more expensive, and it was a need. Material things were optional, but the love he gave her was priceless, and still to this day, she loved him for that.

A girl can never have a big brother as caring and giving as Kelvin is. Kelvin was the only boy, and always very quiet when my father was around. This one event took turns for the better. Kelvin was graduating and my father bought him these shoes he liked, so Kelvin put them on and started moonwalking like he was Michael Jackson. That made him love my father, because his ways of being a man around the house were on point. Becoming a strong, good man made him want to be like my dad. The absence of his father, and the presence of my daddy groomed him to be the wonderful man that he stands to be today. Having a positive man in the house shaped him to great dealings. Not having his real dad around pushed him even harder to greatness.

The smartest big sister a girl could ever dream of looking up to. Nikkeenna was the oldest out of them all, her and my father's relationship was great. He made sure she was never in need, and gave her his love. With him being around, she knew what her future home would be like. When my dad left my mom, she felt as if he had left her, too. It devastated her, because her and Kelvin's father were not around. She had that male role model, but he left her. Time went on, and as she got older, she forgave him and still honored the guidance he provided, not only for her, but what he provided within herself.

Even when it came down to his wife's kids, he treated all three of them as if they were his own. So, of course taking care of my mom's kids came easy for him since he was already doing things for his wife's kids. His love for them was just as deep as it was for his wife, because once he married and became one with her, the love had to be the same for the kids, which they were.

The purpose of my father giving us girls what we wanted and showing us love, was his way of telling us about our worth. The boys all respected my father for providing for the home, and doing things a man should do for his lady. Daddy expectations were out of this world! That is why I am so privileged to have the knowledge I contained from my father when he gave it to me. Women must pay attention to every detail of action a man or boy gives, and a man must not play mind games with every woman he comes across. Simply because the outcome may not be nice.

Chapter 5

Growing Pains

As a woman, I can admit to myself that it was silly of me to say a lady would not become ladylike if her father was absent in her life. I mean, we are entitled to our own opinions, but when you think about it, opinions are only made from our personal assumption on how we view things in our eyes. They are not facts! Growing up as a girl, I had it all wrong. To sit up and judge a person just because their father was absent was wrong. Being the woman I am today, I can admit my wrongful thinking. Was I a bad kid for passing such ugly judgement amongst my friends? No! Simply because I did not know any better. As a child, my way of thinking was based on only what I felt. Within the community I grew up in, most of the girl's fathers were not around. The way they acted was very different from me, and boys treated me better. My opinion became so strong. Why? Because my neighborhood was all I knew, and in my head, I was so much better than the rest of the girls in the community.

Little did I know, my assumptions began to puzzle me a bit. There I was beginning to venture out and hang out with girls outside my community, and I was loving it. We became closer and closer, and I found out that some of these young ladies' fathers were present in their lives, yet they were acting like some of the chicks in my community whose fathers were absent. It took me for a bit of a loop! Here I was, judging one set of girls for acting a certain kind of way, only to find out the set of girls that I thought were so much more, are just the same. Nothing better, and nothing less. I learned that it is not my job to judge any human being. It brings me joy how friendly I've become. I used to walk around like it was Jalisha's world. Tuh!

As I got older, my habits in the dating world were similar to the young ladies I judged so poorly. So, judging is to only be done by the man upstairs, my opinion should be kept to myself. And, as I grew older, my opinions became falser. Not only were others proving me wrong, but I started doing all the things I said I would never do, and my father was still there.

I feel like when telling someone you love them, I sure as hell hope you really mean it, because if you don't, your ass is gon' feel it. Just thinking about it puts this huge smile on my face. My stomach is full of butterflies, and my heart is racing 100 miles per hour. My cheeks are about to break from blushing so hard! This is just how Cortez made me feel.

It all started back at Hill High School in Mrs. Ardley's 9th Grade homeroom class. This chick Tanya was the first person that spoke to me. She watched Cortez the entire first week of school. He always spoke to me, but she never said a word to him. Tanya and I plotted on how she would approach him and let him know she liked him. She was so terrified, because she thought he was so fine and wouldn't be interested in a girl like herself. So, she insisted that I go talk to Cortez for her. I told her she should go herself, because I knew his type, and I didn't want him thinking I wanted his ass.

Tanya begged and said, "Please, Jalisha, you're a pretty girl, plus he already speaks to you."

I replied, "Honey, please! You are as pretty as I am, girl, bye!" She gave me a stern look, and me being the friend I am, I decided to go and talk to him for her.

I let him know my homegirl liked him, and he said "Homegirl who?" I then pointed to Tanya. He said, "What if I told you that I like you and not her." I didn't know what to say because his smile had me!

I blurted out, "Honey, I don't like you, sorry, though!"

He gave my cheeks a soft pinch and replied, "Yes you do." He was so confident. He knew I wanted him. I mean, I did, but I wouldn't let his cocky self know it. All I could do was look back and see Tanya smiling so hard. I felt bad knowing that Cortez liked me and not her. The bell rung just before I could return to my chair.

Tanya jetted out the door so fast yelling, "I'll catch up with you tomorrow, Jalisha!"

Cortez stood in the hall and walked me to my next class. We talked and laughed, then exchanged numbers.

As I was entering the class, he yelled out, "Told you you liked me too." All I could do was roll my eyes, because I was blushing at his confidence, and the fact he knew he had me already.

The next day of school, Tanya and I were chit chatting, and out the blue, Cortez came out of nowhere and hugged my neck, and said "What's up?" to Tanya. Her cheeks were as red as roses! How in the world was I going to tell her he liked me and not her? The bell rang for our next class, but this time, Cortez stood right at the door, yelling, "Mook, come on, shawty!" I looked over at him like, no he did not just call me shawty.

Tanya looked at me and said, "Ohhh, he likes you. I knew he would." She then smiled and continued, "See you tomorrow, friend." I was flabbergasted because she liked him, yet seemed excited to see that he liked me instead of her. I shrugged it off and met Cortez at the classroom door.

Whoever would have thought, 14 years later, we would still be around one another. I had finally found the man of my dreams. Him and I had been friends since 2004, and later decided to take our friendship to the next level in 2012. It seemed as if everything my father said a man should do, he made sure he did it all. By me being so young, I never knew a guy could make me feel this important. He put so much time into me to convince me that he was the one for me. When I saw him, he would just make my heart melt, because the feeling I felt for him was like no other feeling I've ever encountered.

Then I had to realize that all men are not the same. My father told me, "You're single until he puts a ring on your finger." So, that was what I stood by when it came to dating. We said we were in a relationship, but that did not matter to me, because I was young, and knew we wouldn't be together for a long period of time anyway, so it took me some time to realize and accept that I found Mr. Right at such a young age. I continued to play around, but he still stayed right by my side, until I realized, oh yeah, I got him.

His behavior never changed, and that was what made me fall so deep, and open up more to him.

Was I stupid for allowing this guy to come into my life on a more sexual and compassionate level? Hell no, because when I brought him in, I didn't think about the wrong that could happen. All I saw was the love and happiness he brought into my life. That's why when he finally hurt me, all he had to do was apologize. He had never done anything wrong before, and he came to me and sat me down, and filled me in on how he would never do it again. Then, he got back to being the lover he had always been.

Until he did it again, but this time, he didn't tell me, I found out on my own. The trust level I had died down a bit after he cheated the first time. I caught myself doing things I never did. Why was I doing it? Because I was skeptical now. So, going through his phone, checking new locations on where he'd been going, pulling up on him unexpectedly, questioning him to the max, and being around him 24/7 became a routine for me. He had done it twice before, so I figured he would do it again.

You find yourself making excuses for him because you know that he is a good man. Now, when he does wrong, you just shrug your shoulders and wave it off like it's nothing. Realizing over time that you have shrugged your shoulders and waved your hands quite often these days. The behavior this guy is giving is totally unacceptable!

I got so caught up in this crazy chick attitude, and I completely lost myself. Who was I? Was this what for better or worse felt like? The sweet man I fell in love with has now done a 360 on me.

I began talking to myself. Why was I becoming this nagging chick I vowed never to become? We only argued when we were alone with one another, and put on a cool front in front of friends and family, so we could look like the 'it' couple people saw us as.

Then things took a turn for the worst. He sat me down and told me, "We should be friends, because the relationship thing is not working anymore." My heart felt like a brick falling down, hitting the concrete. All I knew was him, and couldn't picture myself being with anyone but him. So, I still didn't let that phase me, and continued to be around him. I still treated him like he was my man. In my mind, I felt that if I stayed around, then I could keep showing him I can treat him better and better. He would eventually realize sooner or later that I'm definitely the one for him.

Until one day I went into my room by myself and came to my senses. Questioning and interrogating myself like I was crazy. I felt like I was in a movie. I went straight to acting mode. Why was I loving this man and giving him my all when we were done? Why did this love I had for him keep making me go against everything my father ever told me? Why was I forgiving this man who cheated on me, lied to me, and made me question my personality? Why did I let my guard down and love him with every part of my body? I knew what I was doing was crazy. He was my boyfriend, yet I was treating him like he was my husband. I allowed him to get too comfortable in the bad habits of being unappreciative of my kind doings. Rubbing his back, cooking, cleaning, buying him things, being one call away every day, and just still being there for him. I didn't want to just be someone he could go back to and fall back on anytime he damn well pleased. I was very aware of my worth and knew what I deserved. What I put in and gave to his ass should have been given back to me 1,000%. At the end of the day, it all came down to a four-letter word: L-O-V-E. Yes, I was in love with him. The love I had for him couldn't vanish overnight, nor could it go away just because he did something wrong.

Right then and there, all the questions that once baffled me, had answers. Trying to hurt someone as bad as they hurt you, is an epic fail. All the energy and thought into so much negativity is so not worth it in the end. Especially when you've gained so much positive through it all. Wise up and leave the past behind you. Only focus on how you will be better for now, and even better in the future.

I knew my daddy would have been a little upset with me with how I chose to handle with the Cortez situation. He even would've asked if I were crazy (lol). Truth be told, I can say I may have been a little wacky. However, it made me understand clearly, though. My dad warned me what not to do, but I had to disagree with what he told me, because I had to really take in and grasp the concept of what it meant to agree.

We have to be true to ourselves and not care about what the next person thinks about our situations. Their situation is not yours, and they will never understand what you're going through. You may have been in the same predicament as someone, but yet again, their situation is not yours. We go through life trying to compare people, this person to that person. Wrong! Here you are, saying this person did this, that, this, and the third, and you wish they could be more like this person, when that person has better qualities that the other person lacks.

Silly, think about it! We all have different DNA for a reason, and last time I checked, it was to differentiate us from the next person. So, what you went through is not what I went through, nor what I've been through. My situation is mine.

So now I understand. You can't call anyone stupid, dumb, or crazy for forgiving a man they once shared so much chemistry with. We have to learn to keep our should've, would've, could've to ourselves. We are so quick to judge others, when all we should do is help them, and try to listen to one another.

I am very grateful my father prepared me for the things a guy could do to me, but my decisions were all up to me in the end. I don't call it letting my guard down now, since I am a grown woman. I simply fell in love with a guy that was brought into my life for a reason, and that was to teach me how to love and be more open. And, no, I know for a fact that he did not hurt me intentionally, because even when we split up, his respect and this bond we grew to have, never died. My present self accepts the fact he was trying to find himself as a man, and I feel like a weight has lifted off my shoulders. Why stay with someone when your heart is not 100%? So, we made the best decision, and that was to go our separate ways. I realized this situation taught me things I didn't know I had in me. I came to common ground. I stayed by his side because we were friends, and not because I wanted him to see me as the woman for him. What I missed was I was already a woman from the start, just not for him.

The outcome became so much better, because I was trying so hard to get him to say, "We gon' do this again." I didn't realize the bigger and better picture that was there the whole time, which was our friendship. He already served his purpose for coming into my life. We experienced so much while growing up together. He also had a child in high school. We were both parents while in high school, both students and didn't have jobs, but still had hustles to be the great teen parents we were. All while maintaining college work, getting our first vehicles, excited that we weren't on MARTA anymore, starting our first jobs at someone's establishment, taking trips outside the states, and planning to visit countries. We allowed our boys to build a bond, and watched them grow through the stages of life, from infants, to toddlers, to kids. We set the boys up a bank account, then worked on our credit scores, but most of all, we were there for each other through thick and thin, no matter what the situation may have been.

I would not go back and change anything, because we both took something positive in the end. I taught him how to have fun, try new things, and spend money. In return, he taught me how to be responsible, save, and most of all, how to love.

In the end, I realized just because him and I were not together, it did not mean we had to hate one another and stop speaking, as if we never knew one another. We have grown apart on different levels, but one thing that we do have that will never die, is our friendship and bond. You cannot be taught the game as a woman, you actually have to play it and see your errors, so that you can beat the next level the next go around.

Fathers, be honest with your daughters and let them know they will get hurt sometimes, but it is okay to love. If you don't, she will end up doing all sorts of crazy things to the guy that she loves. She'll step out of her character, ready to go crazy. Trust me, I know, fellas, and you certainly do not want that. Becoming a woman is one hell of an experience to go through.

Chapter 6

A Daughter's Desolation

I sit here and try to convince myself that everything will be ok, knowing that my heart is still broken. The times that we shared together bring me so much joy, yet so much hurt at the same time. Before I can even think further, my eyes get numb and become overwhelmed with tears. I look up and see the obituary of my father. Tears become more intense as my mind goes off and really takes in what is in front of me. All I am staring at is a piece of nicely folded paper with my father's face on it. At that moment, all there was for me to do was cry my eyes out. My father will never be able to reach out, hug me, and wipe my tears away from my fat cheeks he would always pinch. I gaze back up at the picture and see that crooked smile, and three words that read: Celebration of Life. So, I decide to wipe my tears away, and in the midst of doing so, I hear him say, "Crying don't make no flowers grow, but it is good to let it out, you finish."

I never grasped the purpose of him saying that, not until I was older, at least. Every single time when I would cry, he would say that little saying, and instead of me crying dramatically, I would stop and engage in conversation. I would say, "Dad, how do you know my tears won't make flowers grow, my tears are water."

He would reply, "Never know." And next thing you know, we doing the opposite of anything it was that caused me to cry in the first place. Good way to shut me on up without actually saying it, Daddy (laughs).

Now that same crooked smile on his face appears upon mine.

Chapter 7

A Daughter's Deplore

That is why you never take moments for granted, because you do not know when the time is up for someone you cherish so dearly to your heart.

This is a day I thought would not be here for a long time, but you know, that man upstairs seems to have it all planned out. December 4, 2013, in the morning, to be exact, is when I discovered my daddy's death. Right before he passed, I had to motivate myself to get my mind right so I could pass my Practicum 2 Final Exam in Cosmetology School. Passing it with flying colors was a must, because my dad and I had been conversing about it for weeks. Shaking the fact that he was feeling down in the hospital was a bit puzzling and difficult. If I passed it, I was going to go straight down to the hospital afterwards to give him the great news. I knew that would perk him up. At least, that was what I assumed. When I arrived at school, my classmates were so loving, and we started fixing each other's hair and makeup. My spirits were all up, so I went to the restroom and happened to see a voicemail from Taprine.

She sounded so raspy, and all I made out was, "Dad's not breathing on his own anymore." I dropped my phone and cried my soul out. My classmates ran into the restroom seconds later. They called Taprine so she could come get me. There were so many thoughts racing through my head. My aunts tried their best to calm me, but all I wanted was to get to my father. He needed to hear his baby girls voice, and that would make him breathe as hard as he could. I knew it!

He cannot leave me this early on in life, we just have to get down there in a jiffy. When we arrived, I saw my mom, sisters, stepbrothers, and also friends of my dad's. Now I was angry, because I did not understand why everybody was here before me. My dad was not fucking dead, so what the hell! I immediately asked for the doctors, and they pulled me to the side and said, "I'm sorry, Ms. Gilliam, your dad's liver has shut down and he is no longer breathing."

"Hold up!" I said, "The liver is what keeps your body pumping, and he has been hooked up to breathing machines twice before and made it out each time, so we're not giving up."

They looked at me and said, "Ms. Gilliam, I understand."

I walked off and had to tell my family.

The doctor returned an hour later, and asked, "How long do you want to keep him on life support?" My heart started racing like a cheetah chasing its prey. Conversations my dad and I discussed popped up in my head like 1, 2, 3. Being on a breathing machine was something my father never wanted to happen to him.

He always said, "Hell, folks don't want to suffer lying there like a vegetable. If it ever comes down to it, God will let me pull through when it's off, but if not, baby girl, I'm gone like Jeezy. I'll sleep when I die. If I don't, just let Big Daddy sleep away." A slight smile curved on my lips as I realized I could never go against what my father wanted.

So, I said, "Pull it." My aunt was upset, because that's her brother, and she believed he would make it. At the same time, I also believed that he would pull through as well.

I know the talks we had. The back and forth was done, and the doctor said, "At 9 pm, we will pull the plug."

I walked back over to the area where my family and friends all sat, and told them the time everything would take place. More and more family and friends continued to show up. We had been there so long, everyone began to work on up an appetite, so we all went to Chick-Fil-A to grab a bite to eat.

My best friend, Erica, soon called me. Even though we met in high school, it seemed as if she'd been my friend forever, her and I grew so close. It was as if we were sisters. Erica was on the phone telling me she was on her way down there. We were all done eating when my Aunt Shirley, Tudy, Tweety, Muffin, and Miah had arrived to go see my dad.

Time was pushing close. Nine o'clock struck the clock, but the doctor told me they were running late. In my head, I was blank, I still wished my dad would push through. The doctor came again minutes later, but he had someone else with him. I was shaking like it was below zero in there. My heart was beating so fast. I did not know what to think. He was explaining to me that it would not be a good idea to be in the room when they took the breathing tube out. I couldn't care less about what he was talking about, because that was my daddy, and I was going to be damned if he was gon' be alone. He needed to hear us so he could push harder. The doctor agreed to let us in the room, so we went in.

He finally began to remove the tube from my father's throat, and everyone started yelling his name.

"Jerry, you can make it."

"Come on, come on, it's not your time."

"You're stronger than this."

All of my family's eyes were on Daddy, but mine were on the monitor. My cousin, Bernard, put his arms around me, told me to tell my dad anything I wanted him to know. I finally looked at him and tears flowed down my face at an extreme pace. His body was pumping up and down as if he was gasping for air, when in reality, the air was leaving his body. Aunt Brenda began to sing this gospel song, and we all got quiet, my father began to shed tears. When I saw the tears, I panicked. I was so fucking clueless! As I started to lay my head on his chest, I heard the soft, continuous beep of the monitor. I raised my head up and yelled. I was blank, and saw anger for the first time in my life. I have never seen and felt anger at the same time. I flung open the door, my sisters ran to me, and we dropped down to the floor crying. At that moment, I felt like a zombie, numb to everything and everyone. My cousin, George, hugged me so tight from behind. He let me know he was going to be here for me every step of the way.

It was time for the family to leave, and the doctor brought me a bag with my dad's belongings. Rain was coming down so hard that night, but I didn't want an umbrella, or shoes, or shirts, or hugs, or coats, or anything. I just wanted my dad to get his ass up so we could go.

George was one of the coolest big cousins' a girl could have, all the ladies loved him. Whenever I was with him, women would compliment me as well (lol). George and I arrived at my dad's house, but all I could do was stare. I knew nothing about nothing, and really didn't give a damn about figuring it out or not. He asked if I wanted to get out of the car and talk, but my mouth didn't move. He then walked around to the passenger side, where I sat, and all I remembered was looking in the sky, not realizing how I'd gotten there. I felt arms going around my body, but I snatched away from them. I screamed at the top of my lungs, "I don't want to be bothered at this moment!"

Tears started flowing down my face, and oh boy did my adrenaline begin to race. He grabbed me for the second time, and said firmly, "Cousin, I too feel your pain, I once was you!" At that moment, I realized that he really did feel what I was feeling at that moment. His father had passed as well when he was younger.

We both stood in the yard holding one another. We began to feel wet droplets on our body. But, I didn't give a care in the world about the cold water that fell on me in that 43-degree winter weather. I started to walk away, and he took off right beside me. This weird feeling came over me, as if I felt my cries from inside my body, but nothing was coming out of my eyes. He told me, "Let it out, yell, scream, shout. Let it out with every bit of you, don't hold it in." All I could do was stop and fall in his arms.

His tight squeeze was so comforting, and I did everything he told me to do. I yelled, "Why, why, why, why?" George insisted we head into the house, or we would eventually end up with a terrible cold.

He put his coat over my head as we walked towards my dad's place. The entire time, George didn't speak a single word. He just held me close and tight as I cried. All that rain drenched down on us as if we were in the shower. The rest of my family soon joined us at my dad's house.

Later that night, well morning, I laid down in the bed with my aunt's while they slept. I walked the hallway hoping my dad would tell me to come here, like the spirits in the movies. We would just talk, and he would tell me everything's ok, and he would tell me what to do, but it did not happen. I woke up the next morning and finished my dad's daily routine.

I put on his heavy coat, fixed a cup of coffee with a warm banana muffin, swept the leaves off the porch, and sat there. All I did was sit there and cry to myself. My dad was gone, and everything I had in my head about my career and life was gone. He would not be here to see me accomplish anything.

Chapter 8

Gone Too Soon

Days passed me on by. I was still in utter shock that my big daddy was never coming back. Staying in the house only angered me, for the fact being the times we shared took place all over the entire place. We would cook in the kitchen while talking smack about who could make it quicker, or make it taste better. We watched our favorite television shows, and entertained his many guests that came over. He would always come knock on my bedroom door to check on me, just because, and I would always say, "I'm fine, Daddy, you keep checking on me like I am a baby or somethin'."

He would respond, "Well forget yo' little fat ghetto self." We would laugh, and minutes later he'd come again with something I'd asked for, or just to be funny. That man swore he was a comedian of some sort! So many memories.

He was the greatest love of my life. Staying at Cortez's was so much more relaxing.

It was the day before my dad's awakening. I remember getting into the bath he ran for me, putting on some of my favorite R&B, and just relaxing. All I could do was lie there, listless to all problems, wanting my heart clear from the hurt I felt inside. Tears raced down my face, in a matter of seconds, a loud sorrowful cry echoed through the bathroom. He ran into the room holding my wet body so tight, telling me everything would be ok, and he would be right by my side through it all. He grabbed the towel, picked me up out of the water, and began to dry my dripping body off. He then laid me in his bed. He rubbed and comforted my body as I cried, until I eventually fell asleep.

The next morning, he kissed my lips and asked how I felt. All I could do was gaze at him in his eyes as he played with my curly, long red hair. It took me a while to respond, because this was a feeling that was tripping me out. We were both 23 years old, and this guy was treating me like the women in the movies. He was really there, but before I could speak, he kissed me again and said, "It's ok, my Mook Mook. Your dad may not be here, but I'll make sure you're ok, because that is what he would have wanted." Oh goodness! That made me cry even harder. We continued to lie there, and he just rubbed my body gently.

We finally got up and got ready for our day. He dropped me off at my dad's, and he went on to work. Taprine was already there waiting for me. Her and I had to go to the funeral home to drop my dad's suit off. Once we arrived, the employee was letting us know how good he looked, which helped calm me. He called us over to the room where my father lied in his coffin, that I picked. My heart was pounding and my body was shaking with the tears pouring from my face. That was really my dad in this casket. I could not take it, so I stormed outside.

I was sitting in the car silently, when suddenly I heard sniffling. Taprine and I looked at one another and began to burst in laughter! All while crying at the same damn time. At that moment, we realized that we were trying to be strong for one another. We came to realize that it was ok to console someone when it was needed. The soul needs to cry at times. We did just that.

Finally, we made it back to my dad's place, and there my Aunt Beck and Aunt Brenda were in the kitchen throwing down. My Uncle June was in the living room keeping my dad's buddies' company. People were coming by left and right bringing sodas, cakes, pies, food, money, cards, and all those nice things.

Later that night was my father's wake, and I could not push myself to go. I saw his wife's family across the street loading up in the car. All I could do was take it easy on myself. It killed me because I was the one who had to make sure his body was presentable. Putting myself through that again was overwhelming. This was my night to celebrate my dad's life for the last time.

Mary, Erica, and Jermen were already there. They remained by my side the whole time. Just before people started showing up, I glanced at the room, and went to lay on the bed.

"My dad is gone," I said. I just laid there and cried. Jermen came into the room and didn't say a word. She wrapped her arms around me and hugged me. Soon after, Mary told Erica that I was crying and they all just laid around me. I love those chicks! Their comfort made me feel so much better.

I was wiping my eyes while walking to the front door. The responsible friend who kept us in order and made sure everything was good arrived. Dominique was always prompt. She hugged me and had my favorite bottle of wine with a condolences card. We sat outside. Surprisingly, the fashionably late diva arrived second. Shiquita gets dolled up just to go to the store (lol). Her ass didn't know what to say, so all she said was, "Stop crying." She then smacked me on the butt, because she knew that would cheer me up. Then came the most honest and down to earth friend a chick could ever meet. Tory couldn't believe my father had passed. As soon as she heard, she dropped everything to come over and be with me.

It's hard to come across friends that are dedicated to your feelings.

We all went down the street to order food from Wings the Best. We ordered catfish barbeque, lemon pepper tilapia, fries, coleslaw, fried okra, rice, hot teriyaki wings, and sliders. As soon as we were about to eat, the love of my life came walking in the door. Cortez had just gotten off work. We ate good, baby! Once we were done eating, we started cutting up, dancing, and singing, just to enjoy. Later on, my cousin, Tony, his wife, Jennifer, and cousin, Shay, came to join the party as well. My other cousin, Brittany, was there also, but she's the quiet and calm one of us.

Time passed and it was getting late, but we were still up. Tony's son bent over in front of Erica, everyone started shouting, "Uh oh. You know what it means when a baby does that directly in front of you? You're having a baby girl!" We were laughing and talking smack.

Erica was yelling, "No, no, no!" Right after that, I told everyone to take one shot of liquor for my dad.

Everybody did just that, except for Erica, I said to her, "What's up with that?"

She replied, "Best friend, I'm pregnant."

They all started saying, "I knew it."

We were best friend's, and I felt like I should have been told this, but hey, I didn't sweat it at that moment. I still had a little attitude about it, though. We continued playing cards. We had played our last hand and people became tired. Getting up in the morning was something we all dreaded. Cortez told me it was time to leave so we could lay it down. So, I hugged and thanked my family and friends for coming to be with me.

I had a nice buzz, I would not say drunk, but I was not feeling any pain, baby (laughs aloud).

Once I got in the car and began riding, so many thoughts were running through my brain. I felt unhinged. We finally arrived to Cortez's house. He hopped in the shower, and his mom, Ms. Tiny, came in where I laid, hugged me, and told me whenever I was ready to vent and cry my eyes out, she was all ears. She had always been so sweet, and nothing but kind to me since the day I met her. That really meant a lot to me, because it showed me how genuine she really was. In the midst of me crying and trying to talk, she started crying, and before I knew it, we were wiping each other's faces. She excused herself and brought me back a condolences card. She knew the feeling of losing a parent. Her and I talked and cried together some more.

I went on to take a shower so I would be prepared for tomorrow.

The next morning, my Aunt Brenda called at 5:15 am, so I could get up. She said, "Hurry up, you have to do my hair." I hung up and set my alarm to 6:00 am, and I'll be damned, that was the exact time she was calling again! We laughed, because she was going off on me about getting up, and me getting wasted like my daddy. Of course, I got on up.

As Cortez and I were leaving, rain was coming down heavy, and when we were closer to my dad's house, it became more drastic. Cortez and I sat in the car for two to three more minutes, and he just stared at me in silence. I looked away from him and noticed the rain had stopped completely, so we got out of the car and headed in the house.

I began to tell my aunts about the big 18-wheeler wreck on the expressway that broke the wall. Why? Because I knew they were going to ask what took so long. Traffic moved pretty good, though. I proceeded to start working on their hair, and people were coming in left and right. Seemed as if every lady that walked in the door needed me to touch up their hair or makeup. I ran around the house like a chicken with its head cut off. For a moment, I became overwhelmed, so many people calling, texting, rubbing, asking me if I'm ok.

Cortez pulled me to my dad's room and closed the door. There, he had my dress, heels, tights, comb, makeup kit, and curling irons, telling me to pause and get myself together. I did just that, and when I was done, the limo driver was asking for me. We gathered to pray. My heart was pounding, my breathing was heavy, and my body was trembling so bad. In that time frame I did not know what was happening to me. It was like a movie, people were running to their cars to get out of the rain, but it was all in slow motion.

How did I make it to the limousine? I had no clue. I just knew that we sat there for what seemed like hours. It made me smile to see people pulling over in the rain showing respect to my father.

When we arrived, the parking lot was almost full, and people were still coming as we were lining up. So many damn people! It was time for me to start walking, and once I saw my dad lying in that casket, my body froze, tears were flowing, and I was crying my lungs out. Cortez was trying to hold me, but Nikkeenna came up and grabbed me. She held me so tight. That was the first time I'd ever received a hug so tightly from her. I felt all her love in that hug. People were touching me and hugging me as they walked by. Everyone was just there. All I remember seeing were the men removing the flowers, and tucking Daddy in. Cortez was gripping me tightly, then I felt Taprine gripping my left arm.

"They do not understand," I stated. This was the last time I would ever see my father's face up close and personal in real life.

"Calm down," they said. There the casket was, closing right in front of my eyes, never to be opened again.

The pastor preached a great service about my father, bringing up the time he asked my dad how many kids he had, and my father's response was, "All of them. Once you help and teach a child, feed them, and love them like they are your own, they become yours."

The pastor went on to say, "Now that was a loving and caring man."

It was time for people to stand up and share memories about the infamous Jerry, and so many people got up. I was so pleased. It was then time for me to get up there and read the poem I wrote for my dad. I stood on that platform, raised my head, and tears flowed before I could even speak. I knew I saw lots of cars, but all the seats were filled, and people were sitting in extra chairs. Mary yelled out, "I love you, sister." So, I flipped my hair back to give some humor and read my poem.

Daddy Daughter Love

My daddy was the first man I ever loved. Now he can only see me from the skies above.

We were like two peas in a pod. Daddy and daughter against all odds.

Damn, Daddy, you're really not here.

The dreams I have are so unclear.

Clear in a way, yet clear in a sense, me being me with my word suspense.

Here I am again getting all upset, because you left me alone.

But I don't understand why you left me alone.

I often see you in the rain, as you ride upon the wind. When my path comes tumbling down, you pick me up again.

You wanted to talk the day before you left, but I chose not to, and that was my mistake.

The times we shared and the laughs we had, I will never forsake.

My dad was a magnificent man, maybe a little misunderstood. Maybe I didn't sing his praises as often as I should.

Broadcasting live from a daughter's heart, I dreaded the time we were ever apart.

A man, a hard worker, and a man like no other. You may search and you may dig, but a man like my dad you'll never discover.

Even now when my heart is sad, I still wonder why you left. However, sweet memories of you heal my heart as the years go by.

I know you're at peace, and your soul is at rest. There is no need for my tears, for with your love I am so blessed.

Taprine came up and held me while my tears poured. I walked back to my seat and she then proceeded with her own poem. We both went back to our seats and the preacher began to wrap it up, and gave us a beautiful plaque in memory of my dad. Along with coin-like keepsakes with my father's birthdate.

We then left for the burial site. Once we arrived, people came up to me and let me know my poem was beautiful. The family seated while others stood around.

Time came for me to place a beautiful rose on top of his casket. All I could do was stand there, just stiff as a board. Anger filled my heart. Still standing there while everyone proceeded to their cars. His life was done.

My mom came and told me that my poem was heartfelt. She knew I was angry and did not want to move, so she kissed me. My mom was shocked herself about my dad passing and just gave me some space. However, I felt her love for me over the phone while we talked every single night. I heard her tell Cortez that he was good by just standing by my side, not saying a word, just letting me be.

He put his hand on my shoulder and said, "Let's go." I walked away from my father for the very first time, with tears coming down my face.

I sat in the limo with my head on the window, clueless and famished. I asked Erica to go to my dad's house and start setting up. Our limo was the last to arrive. There were so many people. My dad's wife stayed across the street the majority of the time, I never understood why, because I felt like they should have been with me, comforting me. But, that was how they chose to join the party, so whatever.

Food was in rotation, baby. We had good country cooking, soul food, and cakes down to the drinks. People still were bringing me condolences cards with money. I was still shocked. In the end, people began leaving, so my sisters and friends helped straighten up. It was getting late, so I kissed my aunt's and uncle's goodbye, and Cortez and I were out.

We returned back to his place so we could get some rest. We both just laid there smiling. He wiped a tear from my face and told me to be strong. We both drifted asleep while staring at one another in the quiet, dark room, lit by my favorite smelling candle: honeywood.

Chapter 9

Gone Unapologetic

Death is a very difficult pill to swallow, especially when it's a parent or someone who has raised you since you were a child. The thought of it saddens me so deeply. A person you talk to every single day of your life. Starting from when you were an infant, toddler, adolescent, preteen, teen, all the way to adulthood. At times, they even shared your secrets and told hilarious stories with those secrets. This special human who brought so much love, purpose, and meaning into your life. All the joy has come to an end, because they have found peace.

You'd think they were already at peace, being that every time you two were together, all you guys saw was good times, even when times were rough. So, you wonder. Why or how could they be at peace, when they are not present to enjoy life?

Was I not a good enough daughter? Did I not accomplish certain things he expected me to? Was he still angry at me for becoming a teen parent? Did he see the future and decide to just leave, because it wasn't worth him staying around to see? What is it, Dad? Why didn't he stay here with me?

So much anger, so much hurt, and so many unanswered questions. A trillion thoughts hopped around in my head, how could I not be upset!

I'd catch Mary looking at me all the time, but I chose to act as if I didn't see her. Honestly, I felt she would not understand me. She'd tell people, "My little sister is crazy. She's mean as hell, she gon' break like the crazy people in the movies."

I always blew it off with an, "Ok, or maybe you just bring it out of me, and I hope you're around to see it." Straight cut throat. Then she'd try to talk to me and I would give her a look of disgust. Little did she know, I meant no harm. I knew her trying to reach out was only coming from a good place in her heart. I was her baby sister, and she wanted to make sure I was ok. However, in that time and place, I still didn't care to hear it.

Seemingly, everyone who still had their dad's here on Earth, were my biggest supporters and open ears. So, why can't I be mad? Yes, I said it, mad! This feeling is way past angry at this point! My dad was my number one fan, my hero, my rock, my protector, my go-to guy. How could he not stay here on Earth with me, man?

My son, Jamarcus, loved his granddaddy so much! I can't stand the fact that they won't be able to argue over me anymore. My dad telling him, "You're my baby."

Jamarcus responded, "No, I her baby, granddaddy!"

Dad, Uncle June, and friends said it was time for Jamarcus to learn to play chess, checkers, and some dominoes, since he would be turning 4 in a few months. Dad and Jamarcus did all the fun activities a granddad and grandson were supposed to do. How could he not want to stick around for that, Jamarcus is only 3! He's not going to experience the funny talks I shared with Dad. Why not stay and live this life? I don't understand.

Now, the only way to see Dad is in my dreams. Speaking of dreams, the first three times I dreamt of him, it was more like a nightmare. He got out of his casket and held his arms out, wanting to hold me. No! I knew he was dead, and dead people don't hug the living, Daddy.

Then, in the next nightmare, he came upstairs to tell me he was ok. I knew he was dead in that dream as well. That made me feel a little different. So, I dreamed about him again, but this time, he told me he was ok. He grabbed my hand while we danced to our favorite song. At that moment, I woke up around 3:00 am and realized all that angry grief that filled my heart had to vanish my body.

I understand now. It's not that he didn't fight and gave up on life. His purpose on this earth had been severed. He'd seen and experienced all that life had to offer him.

Yes, I know it was pretty disgraceful of me to neglect and cast out the most important people in my life. But, if we can honestly be open about the situation, I am not sorry. At the time of my grief, I didn't see anything wrong with what I thought, and how I acted. If it wasn't for me treating people so poorly, carrying on so angrily, and just letting the hurt take over my body, I wouldn't have been able to understand what it meant by my dad being at peace. He never would have come to me in my dreams to open my eyes. I was blinded by anger, and it caused me to not be happy for the people I loved.

There is no way you can see happiness for someone else if your heart isn't in a good place. We have to hit rock bottom in order to comprehensively grasp the full definition of life and death. So, Daddy, I'm now choosing to accept your death, five years later. That's right, Big Daddy! May seem like a long time to others, but to me, it feels like a few minutes ago.

That's one hell of an unapologetic healed heart.

Chapter 10

When the Heart Heals

Having a father from the first day you're born, and him looking into your beady little eyes, promising you there will be no need to obtain anything in the world. Simply because he'll have it all for you on a silver platter. That is the most valued feeling in the world, coming from a daughter at least. Then, during your adolescent days, he has his friends come and help you with cheer and dance routines, all because he wants you to be the best at everything. Even though in the back of his head, these are the hardest days, because his baby girl is developing in ways he could never prepare himself for. He knew all along those days would come eventually. Finally, the day comes when you're all grown up, and even when you think the daddy's little princess days are over, they aren't. Whenever you're having bad days, or relationship problems, you go to your dad and he gives you this stare. A stare that feels and touches you so deep that you forget any hard situation that was troubling you. From that stare alone, you feel the love and protectiveness he wants you to always remember you have from him, even when he's far away.

No need to weep just because he's not here physically. The things my dad and I shared will always be held so closely in my heart. The impression a father makes on his daughter will provide the biggest impact on her for the rest of her life. She'll try to spot the great qualities that her dad has, and look for them in her future man. So, her standards will always be set at the top.

Still to this day, I sit and think about all the things I used to say coming up as a young girl. I am 26 years old, and I feel as if I have not accomplished too much of anything. However, I am young and have a lot of years ahead of me to grow. Having a son at the age of 18 did not stop me. I completed high school and went to college to get my Cosmetology license. I should be proud of those two main events that I worked at to accomplish.

What I can say is, having my son was a sign to me. I don't think I could love another human being the way I love my son. Jamarcus brought my father and I back together again! He was basically the son my father never had. The way he showed his grandson off astonished me. He would take him to church to lure the women's attention, take walks in the park with him and play, allowed him to have whatever he wanted, whenever he wanted it, sang and listened to music while he danced his little legs, and my favorite of them all, taught him how to play checkers and chess. At the age of three! Jamarcus would get upset and knock the board on the floor, and fold his little arms every time his grandfather would win. My dad would tell him, "I was kidding, you won." Jamarcus would go to him and hug him. Those moments were priceless.

Now to this day, he looks at me and tells me he misses his grandfather. I didn't think he remembered him, but he does. How could I not know, though? Every chance I get, I remind him of his granddaddy, because I don't want him to forget my dad. He's now at an age where he's trying to understand what death really is. He still doesn't understand why he can never see granddaddy again physically. I tell him to remember the good times, because Granddaddy is in his heart. That completely goes over his head, but he will get it later. As a mother, I try to teach and instill everything.

We beat ourselves up inside trying to make sure we cover all the knowledge our kids need.

It amazes me how we can be our own worst critics. It can be a good thing, yet bad at the same time. Even when you are excelling in the eyes of others, in your head, you are never enough. It all comes with growth, you soon will come to fruition. Stop and enjoy the accomplishments that you have accomplished this far along in the journey of your life.

I know this is what I am supposed to do, but it's difficult.

Losing my father was the most disheartening feeling I could ever live through. All I could do was gaze at my three-year-old son in a mystifying way, because he stood in front of me asking, "When can we go see Granddaddy? Mama, Mama, clean this yard, you know my granddaddy don't like leaves all in his yard. Mama, we have to get them up so I can jump in them."

I remember grabbing his small little body and squeezing him tight, saying, "He sure does not."

I had to wipe my face so he would not see Mama crying. How could I explain to a three-year-old that their grandfather will never be able to put the leaves in a pile for him to jump in, push him in the tire dangling from the tree, take him to church and show off the ladies, and teach him how to play chess, checkers, dominoes, and other fun things granddads and grandsons do. How? This feeling is impossible to cope.

No one feels the same pain I feel. Staying strong is a must, so I suck up my tears like a parched person slurping up the last of their beverage. Even if I am alone, I constantly tell myself not to cry, because my dad is happier now.

Tonight, these tears have my heart feeling a little different. Emotions are running wild. I want to blame anyone and everyone for my big daddy leaving my presence, as well as his grandbaby, the boy he never really had. It is no one's fault, though. Daddy was just ready.

All he wanted was for me to grow up and stop being so careless and stubborn. People, at times, have our best interests at heart, especially our parents. What they have to realize is that we are going to go through what we want, because we have to learn for ourselves. My next move has to be my best one thus far. Who else to compete with than yourself?

The time has come for me to stop making excuses and being so angry about him passing. This feeling that has come over my body is pleasant. Writing has always made me feel exhilarating. Especially whenever something is troubling my mind.

My family and friends were all there for me, but four people in particular were with me every day, and put up with my attitude and angry emotions faithfully. Mary, Cortez, Jermen, and Erica. And for that, they will always have a special place in my heart. It made me feel loved, because their fathers are still present in their life, but they chose to still talk to me and empathize with my situation. There were a few of my friends that I thought should have been more supportive, because they knew the relationship my father and I shared. They were not there, though, so I shut them out and acted as if they did not exist, because of the anger and hurt I had in my heart towards them. I often forget people don't always treat you as you treat them. Me being angry was not healthy at all. My old friends were going on about their lives, while I was constantly reminding myself on how they turned their backs on me. So, I came to my senses one day, and said, "Forget them. I am so worried about them still not being here, however, I have four amazing people with me damn near every day. And if they are not there, they are on my phone."

That special love and concern that Mary, Cortez, Jermen, and Erica gave me topped any bitterness I could have in my heart. They held me, wiped my eyes, and got me intoxicated whenever I wanted to just vent. They showed me that people could still love me like that, even after I cursed at them and said crazy comments, when all they were doing was consoling me. It really means a hell of a lot, and they will probably never know how much that meant to me.

Even to the friends I was angry at, I want you to know that I was just angry, and I forgive you, because I have now forgiven myself. We never forget what people do to make us so upset, so we dwell on it even after we say we've forgiven them. To forgive someone else, we must first realize our faults and leave the past in the past. Stop bringing up what happened so many years, months, days, hours, or seconds ago, because we cannot get it back. In life, we have to remember that we don't go through anything, we grow through everything. Live in the moment and enjoy. If all is forgiven, then we will all be well!

The day before he passed, my father tried to tell me something, but I wouldn't listen. So, guess what? I cannot keep trying to figure out what my dad was going to say to me. My dad laid on the couch, told me he was at peace, and that he just wanted to talk to me. However, I walked away from him and said, "Daddy, you're just talking crazy. I don't want to hear that." He said it again, but this time he called me a mean cry baby and laughed. I walked outside crying my ass off, because my dad really thought he was gon' leave his baby girl. He just knew I would be stubborn and not sit to talk. I can only assume what he was going to say, because in actuality, I will never know...

www.ingramcontent.com/pod-product-compliance
Lightning Source LLC
Chambersburg PA
CBHW030059100526
44591CB00008B/202